Air Force One

CORNERSTONES OF FREEDOM

SECOND SERIES

Brendan January

Children's Press®
A Division of Scholastic Inc.
New York • Toronto • London • Auckland • Sydney
Mexico City • New Delhi • Hong Kong
Danbury, Connecticut

Photographs © 2004: AP/Wide World Photos: 29; Corbis Images: 34, 35, 40, 41, 45 center (AFP), 5, 6, 10, 11, 12, 14, 22, 28, 44 top right, 44 bottom (Bettmann), 3, 45 top (Brooks Kraft), 32 (Tim Graham), 31 (Robert Maass), 33, 38 (Wally McNamee), cover bottom (Museum of Flight), 15, 18, 21 (Reuters NewMedia Inc.), 7, 17, 20, 37; Gerald R. Ford Library: 26; Getty Images/Rick Wilking: 16; Hulton|Archive/Getty Images: 8, 44 top left; Jimmy Carter Library: 4, 27, 30; Lyndon Baines Johnson Library/Cecil Stoughton: 36; Ronald Reagan Library/Pete Souza: 24; Time Life Pictures/Getty Images: 19 (Terry Ashe), 25 (Thomas D. Mcavoy), 13, 45 bottom (Art Rickerby), 9 (Peter Stackpole), cover top (Diana Walker), 23 (White House).

Library of Congress Cataloging-in-Publication Data

January, Brendan.

Air Force One / Brendan January.

p. cm. — (Cornerstones of freedom. Second series)

Includes bibliographical references and index.

ISBN 0-516-24236-9

1. Air Force One (Presidential aircraft)—Juvenile literature. 2. Boeing 747 (Jet transports)—Juvenile literature. 3. Presidents—Transportation— United States—Juvenile literature. 4. Presidents—Protection—United States—Juvenile literature. [1. Presidential aircraft.] I. Title. II. Series.

TL723.J35 2004

387.7'42'088351—dc22

2003023900

1 2 3 4 5 6 7 8 9 10 R 13 12 11 10 09 08 07 06 05 04

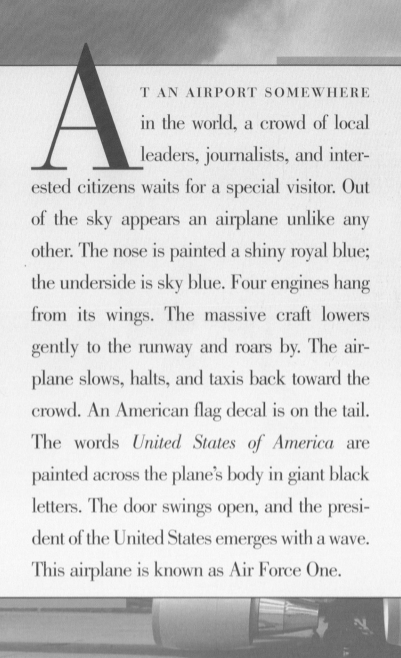

AT AN AIRPORT SOMEWHERE in the world, a crowd of local leaders, journalists, and interested citizens waits for a special visitor. Out of the sky appears an airplane unlike any other. The nose is painted a shiny royal blue; the underside is sky blue. Four engines hang from its wings. The massive craft lowers gently to the runway and roars by. The airplane slows, halts, and taxis back toward the crowd. An American flag decal is on the tail. The words *United States of America* are painted across the plane's body in giant black letters. The door swings open, and the president of the United States emerges with a wave. This airplane is known as Air Force One.

President Jimmy Carter waves from the steps of Air Force One.

The president's job is never over, and each moment in each day is important. The president cannot waste time traveling for several hours. He must always be able to meet with his advisers. He must also be able to fly anywhere in the world and arrive well rested and alert for meetings that could change the course of history.

The president can do this thanks to Air Force One. Part office, part command center, and part home, an aircraft called Air Force One has flown presidents around the globe for more than forty years. It has become one of the most powerful symbols of the presidency and of the United States. It has also been the setting for some of the most important moments in our nation's history. Today, when we consider the importance of this incredible airplane, we may ask, how did presidents ever do their jobs without it?

A decal of the presidential seal, an important symbol of the presidency, appears on Air Force One.

★ ★ ★ ★

TRAVELING PRESIDENTS

Since George Washington (who served as president from 1789 to 1797) first took office, American presidents have recognized the importance of travel. It allows them to see and speak with people, to listen to their concerns, and to determine the mood of the country.

The first presidents had to rely on horse and carriage, which usually meant hours on bumpy roads. This mode of travel was exhausting. A journey from Maryland to South Carolina could take several days. Not surprisingly, most presidents didn't take many trips during their time in office.

In 1863, President Abraham Lincoln (center, in the top hat) traveled to Gettysburg, Pennsylvania, by train. The railroad helped Lincoln to connect with other parts of the country during the Civil War.

In the late 1800s, President Grover Cleveland and his wife traveled in comfort on the train.

Starting in the mid-1800s, railroad tracks were laid. Soon, railroads crisscrossed the nation and knitted it closer together. Travel by railroad was far easier than travel by wagon, and presidents began making "whistle-stop tours." People would gather at each stop, and the president would step out onto the back of the train to give a speech.

Trains remained the preferred style of travel for many years. Though airplanes were flying regularly by the 1920s, they were considered too cramped and too dangerous for presidents. Also, Americans preferred that the president travel within the country, not outside it.

President Franklin Roosevelt (seated, left) and British Prime Minister Winston Churchill (right) met in Casablanca to discuss the progress of World War II.

This changed in 1943, when President Franklin Delano Roosevelt (1933–1945) flew to Casablanca, a small city in Morocco. At the time, the United States was fighting in World War II. Roosevelt needed to meet with the leader of Great Britain, Winston Churchill, to discuss the progress of the war.

The trip took three days, with forty-two hours spent in the air. Roosevelt was exhausted when he returned home. "All has gone well, though I'm a bit tired—too much plane," he wrote to his wife. The first presidential flight was a great success, but Roosevelt made only three more such trips in his lifetime.

* * * *

TAKING TO THE AIR

The next president, Harry Truman (1945–1953), was much more eager to fly. He inherited a **propeller**-driven plane that had been built for Roosevelt and dubbed the "Sacred Cow" by newsmen. On May 5, 1945, Truman rode the Sacred Cow from Washington, D.C., to Kansas City. It was the first time a president had used an airplane to travel within the United States.

Lieutenant Colonel Henry T. Myers was pilot of the *Independence* in 1947.

Truman began flying in airplanes routinely. It was faster and more comfortable than train travel. The Sacred Cow was replaced in 1948 with a new, sleek airplane called *Independence*. In contrast with Roosevelt, whose plane was unmarked so that no one would know when he was flying, Truman had *Independence* painted like a giant eagle. Because the plane had such a vivid design, everyone knew when President Truman had landed. By the time Truman left the White House, he had made sixty-one aircraft trips for a total of 135,098 miles (217,372 kilometers).

The next president, Dwight "Ike" Eisenhower (1953–1961), also enjoyed flying, but he didn't like Truman's plane. Instead, Eisenhower rode in a gray, four-engine propeller aircraft he called the *Columbine II*. It was named after the official flower of Colorado, the state where his wife grew up.

The plane was simply furnished. It had two sofas, two beds, and two large leather chairs for Eisenhower and his wife. Eisenhower kept track of the airplane's progress during a flight by following navigation instruments. He had two clocks placed above his bed, one set for the time in Washington, D.C., and the other set for the time at his destination. There was also a radio above his pillow, which he turned on during long flights to catch signals from cities as he flew over them.

At that time, **air traffic control** and pilots called the president's airplane Air Force 610. Once, when the airplane was flying to Florida, air traffic controllers briefly confused

The *Columbine III*, shown here, was one of two presidential planes used by President Dwight D. Eisenhower.

✴ ✴ ✴ ✴

President Eisenhower and his wife, Mamie, board the *Columbine III* en route to Washington, D.C., in 1955.

CALL SIGN

Air Force One is not an airplane but a **call sign**, a name used by pilots and air traffic control to identify an airplane. Today, Air Force One is usually one of two giant blue and white 747s. This is the same kind of aircraft used by many airlines to fly hundreds of passengers around the globe each day.

the craft with a nearby passenger plane that had a similar name, Eastern 610. It was decided a new name was needed, one that didn't sound like any other. That name was Air Force One.

Eisenhower preferred flying because it was so much faster than traveling by train or by car. But it wasn't until later in his term, in 1959, that he flew for the first time on jet aircraft. At that time, jets were new, and air fleets were starting to replace propeller-driven aircraft. The new Air Force One was a brand-new Boeing 707 with four powerful jet engines. Ike was impressed by its comfort and size—it was big enough to carry forty passengers. Eisenhower watched the crimson glow of a spectacular sunset from

Indian President Rajendra Prasad welcomed President Eisenhower to New Delhi in 1959.

35,000 feet (10,675 meters). It was, he later wrote, "an unforgettable sight."

The jet aircraft allowed Eisenhower to travel around the world. In one three-week period in December 1959, Eisenhower flew to Italy, Turkey, Pakistan, Afghanistan, India, Iran, Greece, Tunisia, France, Spain, and Morocco. No president had ever taken such a trip before, and many countries had never seen an American president in person.

Eisenhower's trip was especially important because the role of the United States in the world community had changed. World War II had left Europe shattered and divided. A new period of conflict began between the United States and its former **ally**, the Soviet Union. This period of **hostility** was called the Cold War. Each country wanted its system of government and society to dominate the world.

Because of the Cold War, many countries came to view the American president as a world leader. Eisenhower knew that he could no longer just stay within the United States. He had to travel, make speeches, and be seen. He had to demonstrate that the United States was strong and that it could compete against the Soviet Union.

John F. Kennedy (1961–1963), who followed Eisenhower, recognized this important role as well. Kennedy understood the symbolic power of the airplane and its name. His advisers used the code name Air Force One when talking to **journalists**. The name was repeated on newscasts, and it has been used ever since.

John F. Kennedy and his wife, Jackie, arrive at the airport in Dallas, Texas, in 1963.

13

THE FLYING WHITE HOUSE

When the president is on the ground, he spends much of his time in the White House. From his office, the president can talk to people around the world. He can call staff members in for meetings and listen to important reports or news. When the president gets hungry, he can order a favorite meal.

The president's job doesn't stop when he is in the air. He needs the same telephones, advisers, and meals that he needs on the ground. Air Force One provides these services, which is why many people call it the flying White House.

A president's time spent traveling must be as comfortable as the time he spends at home. Here, Ronald Reagan enjoys lunch in his private quarters at the White House.

Air Force One has 4,000 square feet (372 square meters) of usable space, more than most American single-family homes.

Today, Air Force One is a Boeing 747, which has been used to transport presidents since 1990. Although many people fly in 747s, the president's plane is different. It is a special model called VC-25A. The interior has been specially designed for the comfort and protection of the president and his staff.

Air Force One is as tall as a five-story building and more than 231 feet (70 m) long. Its wings stretch 195 feet (60 m), more than half the length of a football field. With its four engines, it has a top speed of 701 miles per hour (1,127 kilometers per hour). The average 747 has a top speed of 604 mph/972 kph.

15

President George W. Bush
and his wife, Laura, relax
aboard Air Force One.

The exact interior layout of Air Force One has never
been revealed, for security reasons. We do know the basic
floor plan. The front of the airplane is reserved for the president, his family, and his closest advisers. Just behind the
nose of the aircraft is a lounge, with plush seats lining both
walls beneath a row of windows. On the wall just behind
the nose is a mural of a brown and tan desert landscape.
The couches can slide open into beds. This area is also
equipped with a shower.

Nearby is the president's office, where the president can
sit in a leather chair and work at a desk. The president's staff
works in two nearby rooms. A large conference room, with

Air Force One has enough room for staff meetings to take place even during flight. Here, President Richard Nixon (seated at table at left) talks with his advisers.

eight leather seats and a heavy wood table, occupies most of the space at the center of the aircraft. There is also a guest chamber, a room for the Secret Service, a room for the **press**, and a rear kitchen. The aircraft has six bathrooms.

There are worktables in several areas and places where staff members can set up a laptop computer. Air Force One has eighty-seven phones, which can connect callers to locations all over the world. To handle these calls, there is electronic equipment on the top level of the airplane. The president's calls are **encoded** so the wrong people can't listen in. The bottom level is reserved for storage, including luggage and food.

When the airplanes are not being used, they are stored in a massive **hangar** at Andrews Air Force Base outside Washington, D.C. Security is very tight there. Armed guards from the 89th Airlift Wing surround the airplanes at all times.

An armed Air Force security guard watches over Air Force One while on the ground in Shreveport, Louisiana.

The presidential helicopter, Marine One, lifts off from the White House lawn.

MARINE ONE

To reach Air Force One, the president leaves the White House and boards a helicopter on the South Lawn. This helicopter, called Marine One, is olive green and white. The words *United States of America* are painted on both sides. Marine One flies the president to Andrews Air Force Base. When the president arrives, Air Force One's engines are already turned on.

HAVING A PLEASANT FLIGHT

Air Force One can carry more than one hundred people, including two pilots, a **navigator**, a **flight engineer**, twenty-six crew members, and seventy-six passengers. This number also includes the president and members of his family, his advisers and staff, and journalists. Though Air Force One is large, it is not as big as the offices used by White House staff. In the airplane's close quarters, staff members and the president mix together on much more familiar terms. "It is as close as it gets to a family situation," recalled Leon Panetta, one of President Bill Clinton's top advisers.

★ ★ ★ ★

Each president has acted differently on Air Force One. Some walked freely through the plane, talking with everyone. George Bush (1989–1993) would take off his suit and put on white socks, slippers, and a jacket with a map of the world on it. Ronald Reagan (1981–1989) changed into a pair of sweatpants after takeoff. Jimmy Carter (1977–1981) often flashed a toothy grin in public, but he could be moody in private. After he boarded Air Force One, he sometimes went directly to his stateroom and shut the door. Kennedy often enjoyed the company of his brother's dog, a black Labrador, on Air Force One. The dog roamed freely throughout the plane.

Other presidents spent time getting to know the airplane's staff. Gerald Ford (1974–1977) greeted the pilots before the flight began. He would ask crew members about their families and invite them to birthday parties at the White House. Bill Clinton (1993–2001) roamed the plane dressed in jeans and a T-shirt and would stop to chat or say hello. An energetic president, Clinton never seemed to sleep. He talked for hours, and he loved to hang out with his young staff to play cards. George W. Bush (2001–) also plays games with his staffers, especially board games.

At some point, each president has taken a trip to the back of the plane to talk to the press. Sometimes the president wants to have an honest conversation about a policy

President Clinton enjoys a good laugh with members of the press.

21

or decision he has made. Sometimes he simply wants to charm them. The reporters sit in their seats and write news stories for the next day. Often, these stories are very critical of the president. Because of this, the president seldom takes time to visit the pressroom. Usually, everything is off the record, meaning that journalists can't write what the president says during a conversation. But sometimes the journalists are given information they are free to use.

President Ford answers questions from the press onboard Air Force One.

Sometimes, presidents can get more work done on Air Force One than in the White House because there are fewer people around.

Some presidents prefer to remain in their part of the airplane. It is one of the few times they can be alone. Reagan said he could get more done on Air Force One than in the White House. Without aides constantly interrupting him, Reagan could write personal letters on a yellow legal pad. He also spent hours writing diary entries in a red leather-bound book.

Clinton said flying on Air Force One was often the only chance he had to be away from ringing phones and visitors. "[I could] read the things I wanted to read, and think about the things I thought I needed to think about. I could just be there," he said.

President Reagan practices putting a golf ball around the plane.

Of course, presidents also take time to relax on Air Force One. Clinton liked to play rock-and-roll and jazz CDs in his cabin. He also enjoyed watching the latest action movies. When President George W. Bush or his staff want to rest, they sometimes watch satellite television on a set mounted in the conference room. Bush likes watching baseball, especially the Texas Rangers, a team that he partly owned at one time. Air Force One has nineteen television screens and a library of movies.

RESTING AND EATING

Flying in comfort is very important for the president. He cannot be tired or appear absentminded during discussions with world leaders. John F. Kennedy suffered a back injury in World War II that caused him pain throughout his life. During one flight to Europe, Kennedy was in agony. To firm up his mattress, his aides stuffed it with horsehair.

Ronald Reagan couldn't sleep at all on Air Force One. He planned his flights to occur during the day. When he flew outside the country, he made his crew change to the time schedule in the country where they were going to land. This included meals. On a flight to Europe that left in the morning from Washington, D.C., Reagan made the crew serve dinner rather than breakfast.

Food on presidential flights is just as important as sleep. Each president has had a favorite meal. Kennedy loved to be served steaming bowls of New England seafood chowder. Gerald Ford ate cottage cheese with steak sauce or ketchup for lunch. Jimmy Carter, who came from Georgia, preferred southern food. His dinners were fried chicken, ham with gravy, lentil-and-franks soup, and grits.

Food was not always a source of enjoyment. Bush had always hated broccoli. As president, he decided to ban the

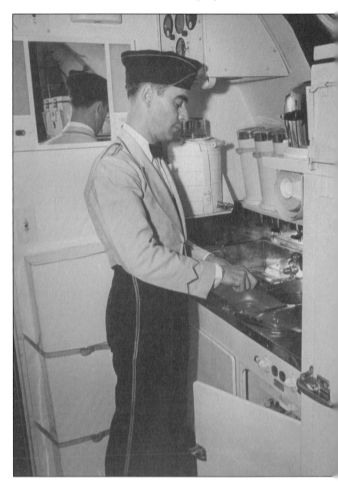

This 1945 photograph shows a view of Air Force One's kitchen, where a steward prepares a meal.

★ ★ ★ ★

vegetable from Air Force One. Reporters later mocked Bush for such small concerns when the country faced pressing issues. Americans often joked that Bill Clinton was overweight from eating fatty foods. Annoyed by the jokes, Clinton changed his diet. On Air Force One, he was served salads and burgers made from vegetables.

CLOSE QUARTERS

Many presidents insisted that their families fly with them. Ford's wife, Betty, often stayed in his cabin while he worked. Reagan was at a loss when his wife, Nancy, wasn't with him on Air Force One. They spent most of their trips alone in their cabin. He even changed the colors in the bathroom from green and white to red because it was her favorite color.

Betty Ford accompanied her husband on a trip to China and Indonesia in 1975.

President Jimmy Carter sometimes took his daughter, Amy, with him on trips.

Bill Clinton enjoyed having his daughter, Chelsea, with him on flights. They sat in the presidential cabin and talked or read quietly next to each other. They seemed so content that the staff didn't want to disturb them.

Amy Carter, the daughter of Jimmy Carter, was one of few children to ride on the airplane. She blasted rock music in her mother's cabin and scrawled crayon marks on the airplane walls.

Amy wasn't the only person to act childishly on the airplane. Sometimes presidents did, too. Air Force One is so intimate, said one journalist, that it's impossible for a

27

President Lyndon Johnson (right) meets with his staff in the Air Force One conference room.

president to maintain a false mood. "If the president is a bully or a lout; if he is generous and kind; if he treats his **subordinates** with respect or disdain—all this will come across on the plane," wrote journalist Kenneth T. Walsh.

One president, Lyndon B. Johnson, was a big man with a big **ego**. In the plane's conference room, Johnson had a special chair installed. He could push a button and the chair would rise, making him the highest person in the room. Johnson's staff called it "the throne." He called Air Force One "my own little plane."

Air Force One has also been the scene of many emotional moments. In 1961, Kennedy flew to Vienna to meet the

Soviet leader Nikita Khrushchev. Khrushchev, who wanted to test Kennedy, bullied the American and refused to discuss anything. After such a disappointing trip, the ride home on Air Force One was like "riding with the losing baseball team after the World Series," recalled an aide.

In the 1992 election, George Bush was facing certain defeat. In the last days before the election, Bush and his staff were on Air Force One. A country-and-western band called the Oak Ridge Boys was invited onboard to perform. The last song seemed to remind everyone that Bush's presidency was about to end. "We were all crying," remembered a friend. "No one said it, but we had the feeling, it's over."

President George Bush has fond memories of Air Force One.

After Bush left the White House for the last time as president, he flew home on Air Force One. He sat in the cabin, quiet and depressed. "On that flight I kept thinking of where I had let good people down—of how I had lost the presidency three months before."

Bush was not the only one to have such feelings. Shortly before Election Day in November 1980, Carter was facing stiff competition from the challenger, Ronald Reagan. Just days before the election, **poll** results came in. They were disastrous for Carter. Carter heard the news on Air Force One when his adviser came into the cabin and burst into tears. "I put my arms around him to comfort him," Carter remembered. It was one of Carter's darkest moments in public office.

Just a year later, Carter was back on Air Force One, though not as president. Reagan asked Carter to travel to Egypt to represent the United States at an important funeral. Reagan also asked Gerald Ford to go with Carter. Carter had defeated Ford for the presidency in 1976, and the two men had not talked since then. On the eighteen-hour return flight, Carter and Ford shared a small room. By then, Carter had also lost the presidency. The two men discussed the pain of their defeats. They shared the difficulties of returning to private life after being president. By the time the airplane landed, they were fast friends.

Jimmy Carter (left) and Gerald Ford (right) became fast friends after a trip together on Air Force One.

A presidential motorcade, or procession of cars, is a familiar sight at Andrews Air Force Base.

Air Force One was also a place for jokes. Reagan liked to walk through the airplane until he found a staffer sound asleep. He would then stand over him or her with an angry frown and have the White House photographer take pictures. Reagan would later send these pictures to the staffer in an envelope along with a letter signed by the president. These images were the cause of much laughter.

AN IMPORTANT SYMBOL

When Air Force One lands, it taxis to a spot on the runway marked by a large white T of tape. The president steps into one of several heavily **armored** limousines. A train of forty to fifty cars carrying press, security, and advisers follows.

31

President Reagan, who had been an actor before becoming president, knew the importance of a good stage. He used Air Force One as a backdrop for his historic meeting with Queen Elizabeth II.

Many say that just seeing Air Force One is an over-whelming experience. Americans and foreign leaders can't help but be awed when the airplane lands and the president emerges. The airplane is a symbol of both power and dignity.

Air Force One can also be the site for embarrassing moments. In June 1975, Ford was walking with his wife down the airplane steps after landing in Salzburg, Austria. It was a rainy day. Ford carried an umbrella in one hand and his other arm was around his wife. Just three steps from the bottom, Ford stumbled and fell to the ground.

Ford's fall down the steps of Air Force One was captured on tape.

"I jumped to my feet, unhurt, and thought nothing of the fall," Ford remembered. But he stumbled in front of dozens of news cameras, and pictures of Ford's fall were beamed around the world. Ford was unfairly portrayed as clumsy and dull. "From that moment on," Ford recalled, "every time I stumbled or bumped my head or fell in the snow, reporters zeroed in on that."

Not everyone likes Air Force One. Operating the airplane and crew is very expensive, and it is paid for with taxpayer dollars. The two 747s currently used as Air

Air Force One reflects the dignity and strength of America wherever it goes.

Force One each cost $300 million to build. Operating those two aircraft costs more than $185 million each year.

But most Americans don't mind. They believe that the president needs to travel in comfort, and they agree that when Air Force One looks good, so does the country. Air Force One is not just for pleasure; it's also for work. In fact, it has been the scene of some of the most important moments in our nation's history.

CODE WORDS

The airwaves around Air Force One are always crackling with messages from security agents. They work to make sure the president is protected at all times. The agents use code words to keep track of the president, his family, and advisers at all times. Here are some of the code words that have been used in the past:

> The White House: *Crown*
>
> George W. Bush: *Trailblazer*
>
> Bill Clinton: *Eagle*
>
> Chelsea Clinton: *Energy*
>
> Jimmy Carter: *Deacon*

FLYING INTO HISTORY

On November 22, 1963, President John F. Kennedy was shot and killed in Dallas, Texas. The assassination shocked Americans, but it was also a very uncertain time. Who was in control of the country? Vice President Lyndon Johnson rushed to Air Force One at the Dallas airport. Kennedy's body was placed in a casket and loaded onto the airplane. Inside a crowded Air Force One cabin, Johnson placed his hand on a Bible and took the oath of office. The moment was photographed and appeared in papers around the world. It showed Johnson grimly

Lyndon Johnson took the presidential oath of office onboard Air Force One on November 22, 1963, just a few hours after the assassination of President Kennedy.

repeating the oath, with Kennedy's widow, Jackie, at his side. A wall of aides was packed into the Air Force One cabin behind them. The photograph showed that, even in time of tragedy, the presidency goes on.

* * * *

Nixon toasts the Chinese prime minister during a banquet in Hangzhou, China, in 1972.

In 1972, Air Force One carried Richard Nixon on his most important trip. For more than twenty years, the United States had frosty relations with China, a giant nation in Asia. By the early 1970s, however, Nixon and the leader of China decided to meet face-to-face. The trip was a great success and opened a new era of peace and understanding between the U.S. and China. It has been called one of Nixon's greatest moments. Though the trip could have been exhausting, Nixon arrived refreshed, and he beamed in photographs taken with the Chinese leader.

Air Force One is also designed to protect the president from those who may want to harm him. In June 1974, Nixon

Air Force One is a safe haven for the president. It can also serve as a national command center in an emergency.

was traveling on Air Force One to visit the Middle East and the Soviet Union. One of the countries on the trip was Syria, a place no president had ever visited before. The Syrian leader sent two Syrian fighter jets to fly next to Air

Force One as a greeting. Unfortunately, no one had told the Air Force One pilot. When the jets suddenly appeared, the pilot thought they were hostile. He slowed down the plane and steered into a steep dive. Everyone on the plane was thrown to the floor. A few minutes later, they learned there had been a mistake. It was one of the only times in Air Force One history when the pilot thought the president was under attack.

Twenty-seven years later, Air Force One had to carry the president through one of the nation's most dangerous moments. On September 11, 2001, a group of terrorists seized control of four American airliners. Two were crashed into the World Trade Center in New York City, another into the Pentagon, outside Washington, D.C. A fourth went down in Pennsylvania. Thousands of people were killed in these attacks. When told of the strikes, Bush boarded Air Force One. For the next several hours, it seemed that anything could be a target, including the president himself. Air Force One flew to 40,000 feet (12,200 m) and took **evasive** maneuvers over the Atlantic Ocean. The pilot had an armed guard placed outside the cockpit door and refused to tell air traffic controllers his exact location. He was worried that terrorists would track the airplane.

Bush was flown to Barksdale, Louisiana, and then to Offutt Air Force Base, in Nebraska. Bush grew impatient. "We need to get back to Washington," he told a Secret Service agent.

DEFENSIVE MEASURES

Air Force One must be able to protect the president. It carries special devices to ward off missiles fired from the ground. It also has a protective shield against a nuclear blast, to prevent the destruction of radios and communication equipment onboard.

"We don't need some tinhorn terrorist to scare us off. The American people want to know where their president is." That evening, Air Force One returned to Maryland and the president was able to return to the White House, where he addressed the nation.

Later, Bush talked about the importance of Air Force One. "It's a majestic symbol of our country," he said. "It reminds me of a bird, the bald eagle, in a way. It's just a powerful look. Every time I see it, I'm proud of our country."

During this time, Air Force One proved its value. It flew the president safely and quickly to where he needed to go.

President George W. Bush steps off Air Force One in Barksdale, Louisiana, on September 11, 2001.

A shadow of Air Force One is cast over the ground.

All the while, he was able to remain in contact with officials on the ground. The government continued to operate during one of the country's greatest **crises**.

That terrible day reminded the American people of the importance of Air Force One. Since then, Air Force One has continued to perform its duty, flying the president in safety and comfort. It is safe to say that as long as there is a president, there will be Air Force One.

Glossary

air traffic control—a station on the ground manned by people who control the nation's air traffic

ally—friend

armored—fitted with special materials to protect against bullets or bombs

call sign—a code word used to identify an aircraft

crisis (plural—crises)—a dangerous moment; an emergency

ego—a feeling of being superior to others

encoded—translated into secret code so that outsiders can't understand the language

evasive—trying to escape danger

flight engineer—a person who helps the pilots fly an aircraft by keeping track of the aircraft's systems and performance

hangar—a large building at an airport where an airplane can be stored

hostility—unfriendly feelings

journalists—writers for newspapers or magazines

navigator—a specially trained person who guides a craft to its destination

poll—a survey about a certain subject

press—a word used to describe the people who work in journalism, either for newspapers, the Internet, radio, or television

propeller—a device that rotates to push against air or water

subordinates—people who work for someone else or are under the person's command

Timeline: Air Force One

1943

President Franklin Roosevelt flies to Casablanca, Morocco, to meet Winston Churchill. Roosevelt becomes the first president to fly while in office.

1945

Roosevelt flies on the "Sacred Cow" to meet Soviet leader Josef Stalin at Yalta.

1946

President Harry S. Truman flies in the *Independence*. He becomes the first president to fly regularly.

1953

President Dwight D. Eisenhower becomes president and begins flying in the *Columbine II*.

1959

AUGUST
Eisenhower becomes the first president to fly in a jet, a new Boeing 707.

DECEMBER
Eisenhower takes a nineteen-day trip to Europe, the Middle East, and

1962

Asia. A new Boeing 707, SAM 26000, arrives at Andrews Air Force Base.

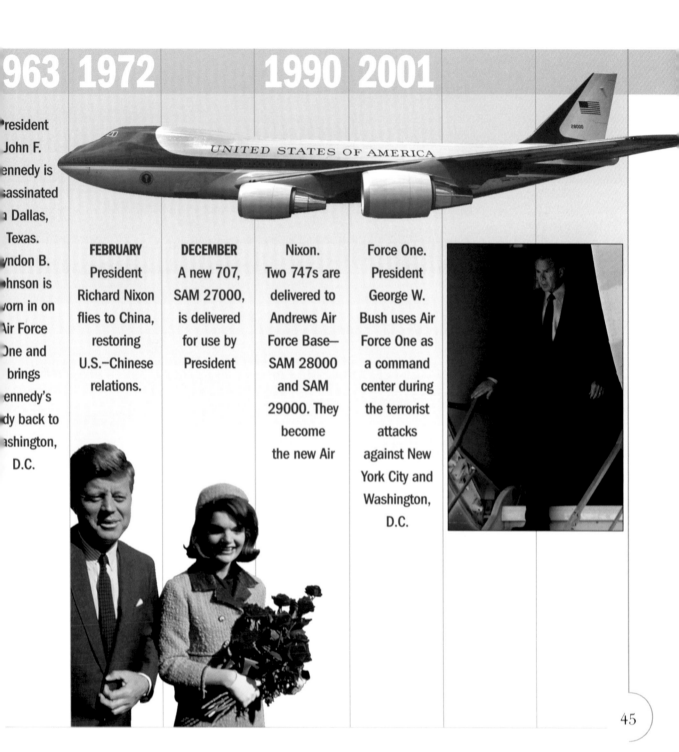

1963 **1972**   **1990** **2001**

President John F. Kennedy is assassinated in Dallas, Texas. Lyndon B. Johnson is sworn in on Air Force One and brings Kennedy's body back to Washington, D.C.

FEBRUARY President Richard Nixon flies to China, restoring U.S.–Chinese relations.

DECEMBER A new 707, SAM 27000, is delivered for use by President Nixon.

Two 747s are delivered to Andrews Air Force Base— SAM 28000 and SAM 29000. They become the new Air Force One.

President George W. Bush uses Air Force One as a command center during the terrorist attacks against New York City and Washington, D.C.

45

To Find Out More

BOOKS AND JOURNALS

Gunston, Bill. *The World of Flight*. Milwaukee, Wis.: Gareth Stevens, 2001.

Hess, Debra. *The White House*. Tarrytown, N.Y.: Benchmark Books, 2004.

Santella, Andrew. *Air Force One*. Brookfield, Conn.: Millbrook Press, 2003.

VIDEO

National Geographic. *Air Force One*. Warner Home Video, 2001.

ONLINE SITES

How Air Force One Works
http://www.howstuffworks.com/air-force-one.htm

Boeing: Air Force One
http://www.boeing.com/defense-space/military/af1/flash.html

Index

About the Author

Brendan January is an award-winning author of books for young readers. A graduate of Haverford College and Columbia Graduate School of Journalism, January is a Fulbright Scholar and a journalist at CBS MarketWatch. He lives in northern New Jersey with his wife and daughter.